A HISTÓRIA DOS NÚMEROS

THE NUMBER STORY

SMALL BOOK ONE

ENGLISH - PORTUGUÉSE

Numbers Teach Children Their Number Names

written and illustrated by

MISS ANNA

Early Reader Edition of *The Number Story 1*
Bronze Medal Winner, 2016 Wishing Shelf Book Award

Cover by | Lumpy Publishing
Layout by | Lumpy Publishing
Translated by Isabel
Coloring by Jieeun Woo and Maria Mirabella

Library of Congress Control Number: 2018902040

Names: Miss Anna, author.
Title: Number story : numbers teach children their number names / Miss Anna.
Description: Portland, OR: Lumpy Publishing, 2018.
Identifiers: ISBN 978-1-945977-19-0 | LCCN 2018902040
Summary: The pictures and rhymes present stories which introduce numbers 0-10.
Subjects: LCSH Numeration—English--Portuguese--Pictorial works--Juvenile literature. | BISAC JUVENILE NONFICTION /
Languages: English--Portuguese
Classification: LCC QA141.3 .M57 2018 | DDC 513—dc23

Publisher: Lumpy Publishing
Website: www.missannabooks.com
Email: missanna@missannabooks.com

Paperback: ISBN 978-1-945977-19-0
Printed in the U.S.A.   1 3 5 7 9 10 8 6 4 2

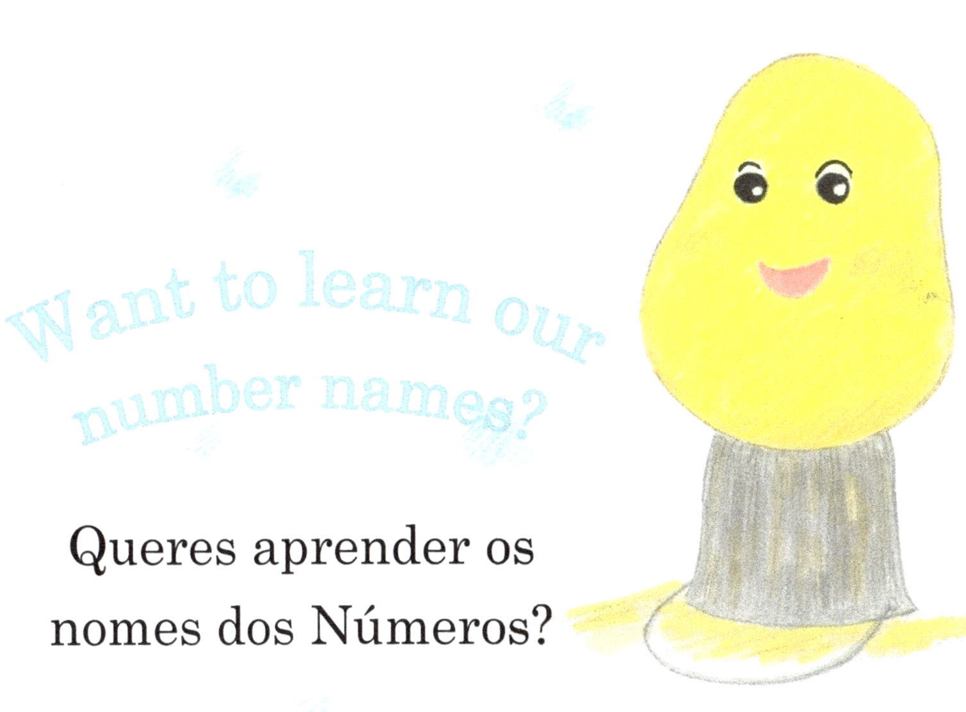

Queres aprender os
nomes dos Números?

It is very easy and a lot of fun!
É muito fácil e divertido!

Say-along our little jingle

Repete comigo nossa pequena canção

starting from Number One!

Começando com o Número Um!

1

ONE looks like my one finger.

UM

parece o meu dedo.

ONE!
UM!

2

TWO trails a tail.

DOIS

gosta da cauda.

A TAIL!   UMA CAUDA!

3

THREE has bumps.

TRÊS

tem curvas.

BUMPY! AS CURVAS!

4

FOUR   carries a sail.

QUATRO

é uma vela.

4
A SAIL!
UMA VELA!

5

FIVE   is a racing track.

CINCO

é uma pista de corrida.

VROOM
VROOOOM!

6

SIX curves like a snail.

SEIS

curvas como um caracol.

A SNAIL! UM CARACOL!

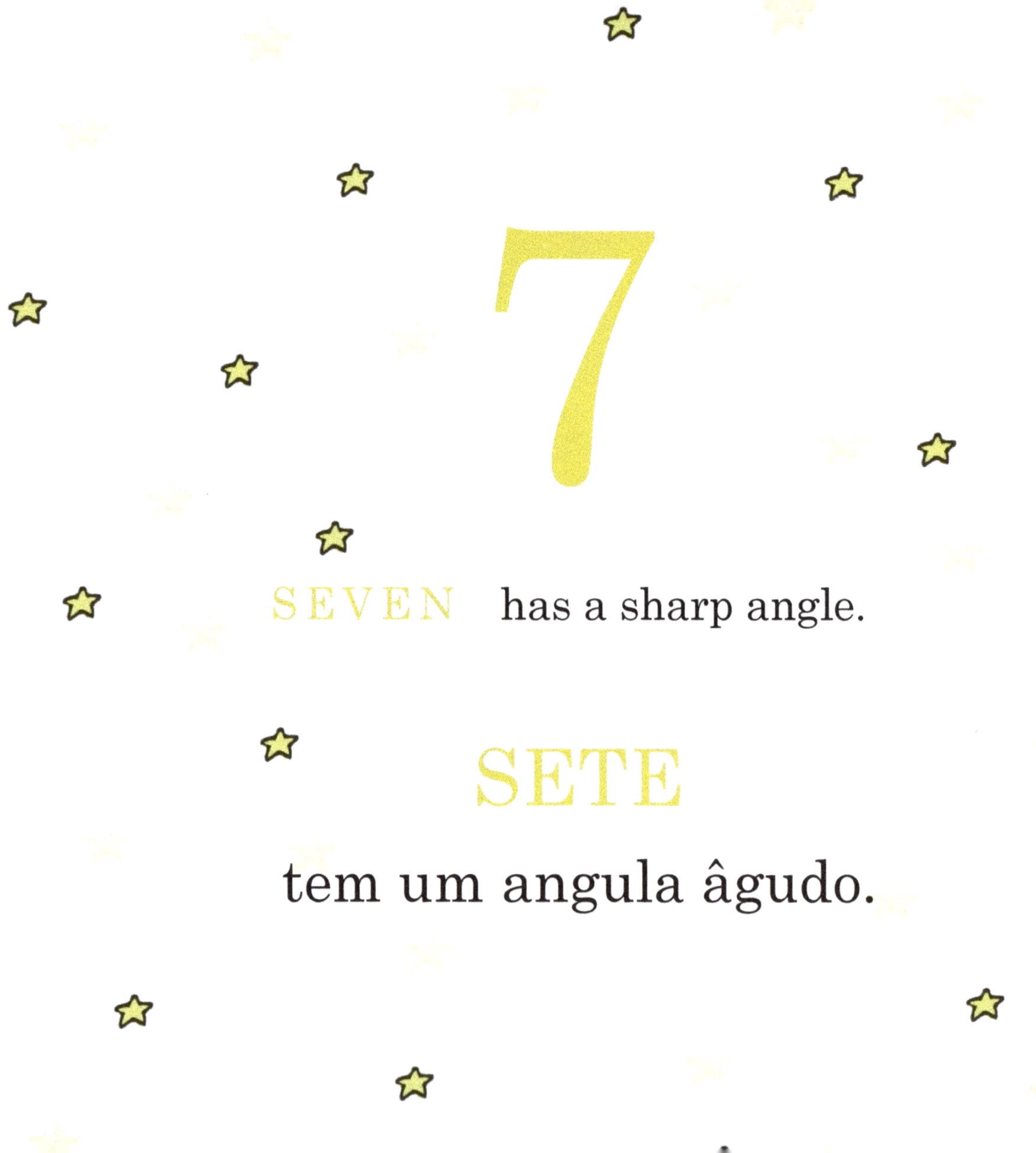

7

SEVEN has a sharp angle.

SETE

tem um angula âgudo.

OUCH!

AI!

8

EIGHT is rollercoaster rails.

OITO

é divertido como
uma montanha-russa.

YUPIIII!
YIPPEE!

9

NINE is a bubble on a stick.

NOVE

é uma bolha bonita.

A BUBBLE! UMA BOLHA!

10

TEN is an eye of a whale.

DEZ

é um grande olho de uma baleia.

HELLO!
OLÁ!

And
E

0

ZERO   is an empty pail.

ZERO

é um balde vazio.

IT'S
EMPTY!
ESTÁ VAZIO!

Thank you for playing with us today.

We had a lot of fun too!

Obrigado por jogar hoje comigo.

Nos divertimos muito!

We are your Number friends,
Zero to Ten,
Who will be here for you~
Somos teus amigos
do Zero ao Dez.
E vamos estar aqui para ti!

Bye-bye now!
See you again soon.
Tchau - Tchau!
Nos vemos mais tarde!